THE HOME OF MARRIAGE

LARRY AND LEENEEN HARRIS

Copyright © 2024 by Larry and Leeneen Harris

All rights reserved. Except as permitted under the U.S. Copyright Act of 1976, no part of this publication may be reproduced, distributed, or transmitted in any form or by any means, electronic or mechanical, or stored in a database or retrieval system without the prior written permission of the publisher.

Scripture references marked (KJV) taken from the King James Version. Public Domain.

Scriptures taken from the New King James Version®. Copyright © 1982 by Thomas Nelson. Used by permission. All rights reserved.

Scriptures taken from the HOLY BIBLE, NEW INTERNATIONAL VERSION®. NIV®. Copyright © 1973, 1978, 1984 by International Bible Society. Used by permission of Zondervan. All rights reserved worldwide.

Scripture quotations marked (NLT) are taken from the Holy Bible, New Living Translation, copyright ©1996, 2004, 2015 by Tyndale House Foundation. Used by permission of Tyndale House Publishers, Carol Stream, Illinois 60188. All rights reserved.

Scripture quotations marked MSG are taken from The Message, copyright © 1993, 2002, 2018 by Eugene H. Peterson. Used by permission of NavPress. All rights reserved. Represented by Tyndale House Publishers.

Any internet addresses (websites, blogs, URL's, etc.) in this book are offered as a resource. They are not intended in any way to be or imply endorsement and does not guarantee that any content on such websites is, or will remain, accurate or appropriate.

ISBN: 9798341077539

Available on Amazon.com and other retail outlets

Compiled and Written by: Larry and Leeneen Harris
Interior Design & Editing by: A Marie Creative Services

We would like to dedicate the work of this book to those who were the greatest examples to us in marriage. These couples gave us the blueprint of what it looks like to be faithful and committed to family. They stood the course without the assistance of family counseling, therapy, or how-to manuals. Many generations are yet standing on their shoulders, and for that, we are grateful.

In Loving Memory of:
Lubirder & William Roundtree, Sr.
Minnie & Watson Harris, Sr.

In Loving Honor of Living Testimony:
Deborah & Nathaniel Davis
Barbara & Lee Carter
Neva & James Jones
Barbara Jean & William Roundtree, Jr.
Meter & Marvin Johnson

DISCLAIMER:

By no means do my husband and I claim to be experts in the field of marriage or counseling, but we have been graced with life experiences that taught us to grow up fast and mature very quickly. Every milestone, hardship, failure, and triumph has had nothing to do with our abilities or capabilities. It has all been because of the grace and mercy of God. There have been tears shed and laughter shared, good times and some tough times, but through it all, we have learned some valuable lessons.

By opening our home, being transparent, and sharing our experiences with you, it is our hope that we can help you avoid some pitfalls and mistakes and realize the beauty that marriage can be.

TABLE OF CONTENTS

Acknowledgments
Foreword
Introduction

Chapter 1.   Marriage: The Husband's Point of View 1
Chapter 2.   Marriage: The Wife's Point of View 7
Chapter 3.   The Terms of Marriage 15
Chapter 4.   The Home of Marriage 29
Chapter 5.   The Yard 39
Chapter 6.   The Garage, The Attic, and The Basement 49
Chapter 7.   The Living Room 57
Chapter 8.   The Kitchen 65
Chapter 9.   The Bedroom 79
Chapter 10. The Nursery 89
Chapter 11. The Empty Nest 99
Chapter 12. The Junk Drawer 107
Chapter 13. The Doghouse 115
Chapter 14. Date Night 125
Chapter 15. Parting Advice 133

Notes
About the Author

ACKNOWLEDGMENTS

The completion of this book is the result of a labor of love shared by my husband and me, inspired by our family, friends, and the commitment of marriage. We are forever grateful for the many couples that have been examples to us.

The content of this book is written in gratitude to our mothers, the late Arnita M. Ashton and Deborah Davis, who always encouraged us to honor the devotion of marriage and family. We thank you for your unrelenting love, support, and encouragement. Our marriage has been able to stand in turbulent times because of your contributions.

"You will never get stronger if you don't lift something heavy."
~Rev. Dr. Marcus D. Cosby

FOREWORD

Sitting here with a thankful and humble heart, I could not help but reflect on the awesome journey that marriage really is. For 23 years, my wife and I have walked hand in hand, both of us navigators together of this windy path called life. It had all its peaks and valleys, joys and sorrows. Moreover, through it all, one constant has stood fast: The gentle embrace of God's love, a beacon of hope even when the storms are at their darkest.

When two young souls first exchange their vows, they encourage it with all the hopes and innocence that are so often used to embark upon some new adventure. Little did we know that the path ahead was going to be filled with challenges, victories, and some moments that would test the very fabric of our commitment. Looking back, it is the struggles through which we have formed stronger bonds as friends, and these are the struggles through which we have been able to grow and let each other do things that we would never be able to do on our own.

On some occasions, I felt the globe grow huge, along with many obstacles that could never be overcome. Then, our minds began to accommodate God's gentle voice that surrounded us with love and led us back to understanding and compassion. His love had the power to repair all the tears in our hearts, open the path to light and illuminate our path every day, and make our vows lively and heartwarming.

Through the years, I gained a strong understanding not only of who I am but also of how to mature and how to heal from the world's imperfections. I have a firm belief that marriage as a male is not only about supporting each other in our journey through life but also about being the only source of hope and love for each other, such that nothing from the universe can break this covenant unless it's our own decision. As a result of the challenges, I came to understand that our challenges are the places of change, transformation, as well as enlightenment regarding what true unity is in the real sense.

~ *Rev. Brandon J. Owens Sr.*

This unity [of marriage] purports to be physical; it must be spiritual and finally purposeful. I have witnessed the power of forgiveness, being strong enough to leave our worries and uncertainties to the Lord, and having a deep faith that enables a loving attitude to win all the battles. Through my experience as a wife, I have become aware of how gently God holds a soul in his embrace, a holy brow under which he changes the very darkest night into a blue dawn.

Even the best of couples, whether you're dating, married, or divorced, may find themselves saying, "Why didn't anyone tell me that?" When it comes to relationships, there's often certain things we just don't talk about. The one you feel you should be able to talk to may be the one who hurt you. You may feel like you won't be heard or taken seriously, so you just hold your feelings in. Perhaps, we don't want to hurt our significant other's feelings by being honest or we are too shy or we don't know the words to say because we haven't been taught how to communicate. No matter what the reason, any successful relationship will always consist of communication.

At 13 years old, I met my now husband, I didn't know anything about being in a relationship, not primarily because of my age, but I didn't see an example of a healthy relationship at home. Unfortunately,

FOREWORD

this is probably the story of many. So as time went on, I learned by many trials and errors.

Now, after 23 years of marriage and four children later, I have experienced many things, and I found myself saying, "I wish I would have known earlier what I know now."

~ *First Lady Shamia Owens*

Fortunately for you, with the guidance and vision from these wonderful authors, Leeneen and Larry Harris, you will begin to see the reality in this book, The Home of Marriage. They have shared some of their experiences in hopes that you will find your safe space with the one you have chosen to be committed to. They have shared many personal relationship nuggets in hopes that it will help you navigate the aspects of your relationship, whether dating or married. It is our hope that this book will begin to open a line of conversation with your partner that solidifies a more in-depth understanding of you as an individual and as a couple. It is worth the time to discover each of our places in The Home of Marriage.

Rev. Brandon J. Owens Sr. & First Lady Shamia Owens
Bethel Missionary Baptist Church
Longview, Texas

INTRODUCTION

In these millennial times, marriage is a foundation that many deem as an antiquated practice. It is often looked at as an optional custom. For the remainder of us who celebrate and appreciate the institution of marriage, we have found that it is not simply a custom or tradition; it is a conscious decision and commitment.

Marriage is more than "once upon a time" and "they lived happily ever after." The alliance of marriage is hard, consistent work. It cannot be simmered down to flowers, cake, tuxedos, and a designer wedding dress. It is much more than that. The altar is where many marry with an idea of what they have imagined in their mind. They have imagined what they want their spouse to be and what their spouse should look like. However, they have not imagined the reality of who their soon-to-be spouse really is.

A key component of marriage is knowing completely who you will be sharing vows with. The reality is, you are marrying everything that your future spouse is and is not. It is imperative that you spend quality time with your future spouse before the vows. The more you know about the one you choose to marry, the better.

Fortunately for us, we were blessed to be friends in the beginning of our relationship. This allowed us to grow as covenant partners, lovers, and ultimately as great friends. We learned together that marriage is honorable, respectable, admirable, and a credible commitment.

Our current society has fantasized and romanticized the tradition of marriage. It has summed up this way of life with many unrealistic ideas. Many go to the altar and pledge "I do until I don't" instead of "I do until death do us part."

The rite of marriage can be a rewarding way of life, but this is all contingent on the mindset of those who enter it. It should not be entered into lightly or half-heartedly. It is a lifelong commitment and not designed for the faint of heart or those who are not committed to staying dedicated to this way of life.

We want to encourage you to stay the course. *It is worth it.* We hope that, through this book, you are able to gather some essential nuggets to help you along your journey to marriage or to enhance those who have already plunged into this blessed agreement.

Note about Reflections: At the end of every chapter, we invite you to take the opportunity to reflect on the content that has been shared. For each reflection, answer individually first. Then, discuss your answers with your partner and discuss your discoveries. If you notice any areas of deficiencies, come up with solutions as a couple and be willing to compromise if necessary.

THE HOME OF MARRIAGE

Chapter 1
Marriage: The Husband's Point of View

I was raised by a single mother who taught me and my brother the value of responsibility. I watched her work hard to provide for our household, and she constantly stayed on us about saying and doing the right thing. She held us accountable for every decision we made.

My mother was the model of a good woman, and she taught me the value of the kind of woman I should have in my life. I didn't need someone to cook and clean for me. Fortunately, in my household, boys washed dishes, washed and ironed clothes, and learned how to cook. My mother wanted to make sure were equipped to live on our own by the time we left home. Because of this, I knew at an early age the kind of woman I wanted to share my life with, and there was no doubt in my mind that I would be a husband one day—and a good one.

As I was starting my junior high school years, I noticed a certain young lady that caught my attention. Although I never approached her, we would always seem to cross paths. For example, we shared a science class, and only one person sat in between us. I tried to get the guy to switch seats, but the teacher would not allow us to do so. The young man wasn't having it either. I think he wanted that coveted seat next to my future queen as well.

As time went on, we often crossed paths, but I was too nervous to speak with her. For example, one Sunday morning, while leaving my grandparents' house, we drove by her as she was walking to church. For some strange reason, I looked back and realized she was also looking at me. That was the first indication that she had noticed me, but I wasn't ready to act on it. Sometime later, while on my way to school, I walked right past her, but I was still afraid to speak or say anything to her.

The fateful moment came when my best friend, Mweusi Lumumba Willingham, called and asked me if I wanted to go to a birthday party with him. I agreed, not knowing whose party we were going to.

Get this. We got to the party, and it was her party! When I saw her, I knew that I was not going to miss another opportunity to say something to her. So, I walked up to her and wished her a Happy Birthday. She smiled and said thank you, and that smile she gave me melted my heart. I could tell she was happy I had come.

As the party went on, I finally got the nerve to ask her to slow dance. She said yes, and we danced together for the rest of her party. Before I left, I asked for her phone number, but it took me two to three days before I could build up enough confidence to call her. When I finally called her and she realized who I was, she dropped the phone and started screaming, "It's him!"

That was the summer of 1982, going into our freshman year of high school. We started dating and have not looked back. I can honestly say I knew I had found my queen, and we have been together for 42 years with 32 years of marriage. We are still living our best life!

To my brothers who have a desire to be a husband one day, my advice and first rule of thumb is to pray for your future wife and for what you need in a wife. Pray that when you recognize her, you have what she needs in a husband. I would also caution you that if your only desire to have a wife is for her to be a glorified maid or sex partner, you are sadly missing the beauty of having a true soulmate and better half.

Marriage is when two individuals declare their love for each other not only in the presence of family and friends but also in the presence of God. It is a spiritual connection—a bond between two souls that is eternal. When a man finds a wife who has the characteristics of respect, loyalty, and integrity, he can build a foundation that leads to a solid marriage, one that is viewed as a divine partnership and not a life sentence of bondage.

As a man, the most important thing you can do to prepare for accepting a wife in your life is to learn to be vulnerable. Most men think being vulnerable is being weak, but true strength is shown through transparency and vulnerability, especially as a husband. Vulnerability requires courage and trust, and when you are vulnerable in marriage, it allows you to create a deeper, more anchored relationship with your wife. Initially, this was hard for me, but when I came to know Jesus Christ as the Lord of my life, it allowed me to see my wife as God sees her. I not only developed empathy, but I also cultivated a forgiving heart, which allowed me to look past her shortcomings and mistakes as well as my own.

The Husband's Point of View...From the Word of God

> *"Who can find a virtuous wife? For her worth is far above rubies. The heart of her husband safely trusts her; so he will have no lack of gain. She does him good and not evil all the days of her life."*
> *~Proverbs 31:10-12 (NKJV)*

A virtuous woman has or shows high moral standards, and you can trust her word. She is reliable and leads her home with integrity and discipline. A virtuous woman has faith in God, and she honors God and fears Him. She is indeed a helpmate to her husband.

This scripture is so befitting of my wife because she has been a trustworthy and valuable part of my life throughout the many years we have been together. When we began dating, I knew she was the woman that I wanted to share my life with, and her actions throughout the years allowed me to develop a trust like I had never known before. Her track record has proven she is trustworthy, she has shown me she's trustworthy, and I vowed to be the same for her.

My wife reminds me of the Proverbs 31 woman. Her character helped cultivate in me the desire to protect her and what we have at all costs. All my needs are met with this one woman, and I don't desire or need anyone else. Let me be clear, she has her faults and quirks, but at the end of the day, I know she fights for what we have and for the family we have built.

The virtuous qualities I recognized in my wife attracted me not only to her outer beauty but to her inner beauty and heart as well. It was in the way she carried herself, her love for God, her love for me, and how she treated family and friends. When you witness someone with that level of dedication, it leads to the kind of deep trust explained in Proverbs 31:11.

> *"He who finds a wife finds a good thing, and obtains favor from the Lord." ~Proverbs 18:22 (NKJV)*

There are two important things a man needs in a relationship: respect and loyalty. When you recognize those two qualities in your spouse, you know you have been blessed with a "good thing," and that, to me, is favor with the Lord.

A wife is a support to her husband in every way, and anything is possible when you are in a marriage that is favorable to every area of your life. For example, I look forward to coming home after a stressful day of work because my wife's positive presence grounds me. Her beautiful smile and her warm and gentle tone make me forget about the crazy day I had outside of our home. I know that, regardless of the day I have had, she will help me refocus on what's most important. My wife ensures that I know she is on my side and has my back through all the ups and downs, and this has encouraged me to be my best self in every area of my life.

I understand that her presence can determine peace or chaos, so I treat my wife with love, honor, and respect because I want the favor of the Lord not just on my life but on both of our lives. The level of commitment, support, and dedication my wife has exemplified allows me to see her as a "good thing," and I cherish her because she is one of my precious gifts from God on earth.

> *"Husbands, Love your wives, just as Christ also loved the church, and gave himself for her; that he might sanctify and cleanse her with the washing of water by the word, That, he might present her to himself a glorious church, not having spot, or wrinkle, or any such thing; but that she should be holy and without blemish. So husbands ought to love their own wives as their own bodies. He who loves his wife loves himself. For no one ever hated his own flesh; but nourishes and cherishes it, just as the Lord does the church." ~Ephesians 5:25-29 (NKJV)*

Men are natural protectors. I vowed that I would do anything and everything to protect my wife, that I would sacrifice whatever it took to keep her safe, to help her, and not harm her in any way (physically, mentally, or verbally). I have to say that sacrifice can be a difficult task. You may have to sacrifice preferences or what you may feel, all for the greater good of your relationship. It may be as simple as agreeing with your spouse's favorite restaurant or as important as where you will live for the next 30 years. But when you realize you don't have the capacity to do it without the Lord's help, it makes you view sacrificing differently.

Sacrificing is oftentimes partnered with compromise. Husbands and wives must sacrifice their time and resources for a healthy relationship because it is imperative that your spouse knows that nothing is more important than what you have together.

Early on, I realized that there were past versions of me that had to be done away with (sacrificed) if my intentions were to have a successful relationship and marriage. Once I discovered the love that God has for me, I then knew how to love myself and anyone connected to me, especially my wife.

To truly love yourself and others is a hard task to do outside of the love of God. When we love on our terms, it is temporary, and many times it comes with conditions. When we experience love God's way, we learn to love ourselves, our spouses, and others as God has intended.

"Husbands, love your wives and do not be bitter toward them."
~Colossians 3:19 (NKJV)

If I could give one final word of advice, it would be to never go to bed angry. You are the king of your castle (your home), and it is your responsibility to make sure that everything is secure inside and outside of your home. If there were a disturbance, you would be expected to address it. The same goes for problems that arise between the two of you.

Bitterness leads to being resentful, and that is a place that we try to stay away from if at all possible. You can avoid feelings of bitterness simply by voicing any unpleasant feelings you have with your spouse as soon as you experience them. Communication is the key to avoid falling into bitterness pitfalls, and you should fix whatever issues that occur inside or outside of the castle...no matter what.

Chapter 2
Marriage: The Wife's Point of View

The question is often asked, *What do you look for in a husband?* The last I checked, from a biblical perspective, there is no specific passage that states that the wife is to look for or seek out a husband. As my husband stated, Proverbs 18:22 says, " He who *finds* a wife, finds a good thing and obtains favor in the Lord." The husband should **FIND**, and the wife should just **BE**.

A wife should, first of all, BE the woman that a husband would look for. In other words, you should work on every aspect of your life that would be attractive to a potential husband. That means taking care of yourself—body, soul, and spirit. This is not just limited to your outward appearance, but it applies to your heart and emotions, as well as your health and finances. When you enter marriage, you should be whole, not just fragments of yourself.

I am well aware that there are many instances where a woman will not have a positive example of what she wants in a husband, whether it's because she was brought up by a single mother or if the father figure was just absent for whatever reason. Then, there are those who have the privilege of being raised around parents and grandparents who have cherished being in a faithful marriage for decades. Either way, one would be able to surmise from the absence of an example or from a great example what type of partnership would be beneficial to them.

When it comes to meeting my husband, I recollect the same events as he does. Larry and I shared a mutual friend named Mweusi. Larry met Mweusi at the neighborhood YMCA at 12 years old, and I met Mweusi when I started Junior High school at 13 years old, and we had some classes together.

It is important to mention Mweusi because he is our friend and brother. He is the reason why we met, and he is responsible for our original connection. Mweusi has witnessed a lot of our life together, and the three of us are all still friends today.

My husband and I officially met at my 14th birthday party, although I had noticed him around school before the party and we had a science class together. It was hard not to notice him because he was a charming, attractive athlete who dressed really dapper, and he always smelled very good. I first noticed how good he smelled when he passed by me one morning as I walked to school.

We always seem to have people in common. He had a group of friends that we later discovered were also my friends. So, it was inevitable that we would eventually meet.

That year, my birthday was on a Wednesday, so we had a birthday party the following weekend. I was extremely excited about my party for many reasons, one being that it was the first party that I was allowed to have that included more than my brothers and cousins. The party was also like an official send-off for me, as I was going from junior high school to high school. So, when Mweusi asked if he could bring a friend to my party, I had no idea it would be the guy I secretly liked—the one I thought was cute and who always smelled so good.

When Mweusi and Larry arrived at my party, the level of excitement I had inside went up several notches. We all exchanged pleasantries and began enjoying hanging out at my party. Then, Larry asked me to slow dance, and that's where it all began for us.

MARRIAGE: THE WIFE'S POINT OF VIEW

Larry and I talked to each other as we danced, and I recognized that he was as nervous as I was. This was the first time that I had ever danced with a boy like this. My previous dances were around the house on Saturday mornings with my Aunt Ruby and Uncle Rod as we listened to old-school music and cleaned the house or when I was clowning around with my brothers, doing the latest moves. I wasn't sure of everything to do, but it seemed like he was sure. He held me so tight, and he smelled even better being this close to me. Needless to say, this was the best party ever! I gave him my phone number and waited for him to call.

I remembered the exact day he called me—June 8th. I remember because I was low-key offended because it took him so long to call.

After the initial excitement of hearing his voice, we talked for hours. This became a daily event for us, and then we began walking home from school together. This is where we really began solidifying being a little couple in puppy love. These were the sweetest and most innocent times of our relationship. We really got to know each other, and we became close during that season of our lives.

When we became juniors in high school, we encountered our first challenge when my family moved out of the district and I had to go to another school. We continued to date each other, but it was hard.

I was able to return to the district during my senior year of high school when I went to stay with my grandma and grandpa, and we graduated high school. In the fall of 1986, we both attended Northwestern State University in Natchitoches, LA. It was in this small town of Louisiana that we really experienced growing up and the challenges of adulting.

As we were going into our sophomore year, we discovered that I was pregnant. Yes, pregnant. This was not how we pictured our fairy-tale life together, but this was our hard reality—the reality of a baby in the mix of us trying to find our way and the reality that life would not be the same for us.

Larry and I navigated the tough waters of having a child, and we married on March 21, 1992. We did put the cart before the horse by having a baby before marriage, but by the grace and mercy of God, we were able to understand that this reality did not define who we would be for the rest of our lives. We have flaws and events in life that happen because we are mortal, but God does not make mistakes. God took a situation that was capable of destroying a couple's relationship and used it to bless our union, and now, we can say that everything we experienced was all for our good.

When I thought of my life as a wife and my idea of marriage, my maternal grandparents always came to mind. I witnessed how my grandmother catered to my grandfather and anticipated his needs. When I entered my own marriage, I wanted to treat my husband in a similar fashion. I wanted to be there for whatever my husband would experience in our home life and outside of the home. I wanted him to know that our home, our castle, was a safe space for whatever he may be experiencing in whatever phase of life we were in.

Too many times in marriage, a spouse may feel comfortable sharing how they truly feel with others (like friends or family) and not their own spouse in fear of hurting their spouse's feelings or in fear of their feelings making them look weak or insufficient. It's a common hurdle, but your spouse must be confident that whatever they are experiencing in life, they can trust you to uphold them and not discredit where they are.

The commitment of marriage is not based solely on meeting the physical needs of your spouse, but it is also of a spiritual and emotional nature. Your spouse must feel assured that their connection with you is secure and that no one is able to penetrate or "put asunder," as the vow states, what God has joined together.

When I thought about the health and wellness of my marriage, my goal was not only to be there for the physical needs of my husband but to be someone he could count on in the good times and happy times, in the not-so-good times, and in the times of struggle.

The Wife's Point of View...From the Word of God

"For wherever you go, I will go; And wherever you lodge, I will lodge; Your people shall be my people, And your God, my God."
~Ruth 1:16(b)

I must say, things didn't start out quite that simple. When we first started out, we were polar opposites. I was the church girl whose whole life centered around church events. I was raised in a traditional Baptist church, and my husband was raised Methodist. It took us a few years to get on the same page when it came to our beliefs, but my prayer was, if he is saved and loves the Lord with all his heart, I know he will love me the way that he is supposed to. As we began to grow together spiritually, I could see the Lord teaching him how to love me and lead me and how to be a good husband to me.

As time went on, my husband, on many occasions, had proven to me that wherever we went in this world, he was my covering, my protector, and my security, and he would provide what our family needed to be healthy and whole. This made it easy for me to trust him wholeheartedly and be confident that if we decided together where we went or where we lived, he would ensure that we, as a family, would be protected.

"Wives, submit to your own husbands, as is fitting in the Lord."
~Colossians 3:18 (NKJV)

We will discuss the subject of submission more later in the book, but in order for you both to enjoy a healthy relationship with each other, mutual submission should not be a dirty word. The man submits because he understands his position and responsibility to God. The woman is able to submit because she sees the man's sacrifice and obedience to God.

THE HOME OF MARRIAGE

Sometimes, in newer marriages, because complete trust has not been established, one spouse or the other may take advice from an outside source like parents, family members, or friends. It's great to have those outside help guide the both of you in difficult situations, but in submitting to your spouse, you cannot allow outside sources to override any decision that is made by you or your spouse. When you both decided to come together as one, that agreement bonded everything about both of you together. Whatever is done or experienced by one will be experienced and felt by the other. It is this bond that leads you both to a relationship of trust and mutual submission.

Submitting, as a wife, means that I trust my husband's word, his decisions, and his direction, and I had no problem submitting to him because of the expressed love he has for me. I know whatever age and stage we may be in, he has my best interest at heart, as well as the best interest of our family.

I have seen over the years how dedicated my husband has been in building our family. When I was a broken little princess, he loved me into becoming the Queen of The Harris home. I will forever be grateful for my best friend, my prayer partner, my protector, my covering, my safe place, the gatekeeper of our home, my husband, my King.

> *"Two people are better off than one, for they can help each other succeed. If one person falls, the other can reach out and help. But someone who falls alone is in real trouble. Likewise, two people lying close together can keep each other warm. But how can one be warm alone? A person standing alone can be attacked and defeated, but two can stand back-to-back and conquer. Three are even better, for a triple braided cord is not easily broken."*
> *~Ecclesiastes 4:9-12 (NLT)*

MARRIAGE: THE WIFE'S POINT OF VIEW

One of the things I had to learn early on in marriage was I was no longer a solo act. As a single person, I was used to doing things alone and depending on myself to get things done. When we became married, we had to rely on each other's ability and thought processes. I had to consider how my husband would feel in certain situations, and he had to do the same for me.

You should always consider your partner and understand that each of you has a role in the partnership. I started to understand this is how a good partnership and marriage should work, like a fine-tuned instrument, in unity and on one accord in any life decision. We accomplished more together, and it didn't take long to make progress when we were on the same page and doing it as a team.

> *"Instead, be kind to each other, tenderhearted, forgiving one another, just as God through Christ has forgiven you." ~Ephesians 4:32 (KJV)*

In the process of learning to mutually submit, you should be willing to forgive often, without conditions and stipulations. None of us are perfect and will make many mistakes, but you should always be open to giving your spouse grace for the things they may get wrong. You should also be willing to hold yourself to the same standards that you are expecting from your spouse. If you don't want a spouse to lie and cheat in the relationship, neither should you lie and cheat.

Chapter 3
The Terms of Marriage

ACCEPTANCE: Accepting the good, bad, and the ugly seems like an old cliché, but it is so true when it comes to marriage. Whatever issues or shortcomings your partner may have become your issues as well. This type of commitment is described in Ephesians 5:31, where it tells us that a man leaves his father and mother and joins with his wife, and the two become one. This is where we see that the things that affect your partner will affect you because the two of you are one. If you are not affected by what affects your partner, you may want to check your intentions for the person you have chosen to commit to.

My husband and I had many things in common with each other, but we also had some things that were totally opposite. My husband, in the beginning, was the more social one in the relationship. He would go out and party with friends and have a liquid libation or two, but I didn't judge or condemn him on what he thought was fun at that time in his life. I just always asked that he not allow his socializing to affect the peace and harmony of our home.

Eventually, my husband came to a place where he realized his socializing was not beneficial to the end goal that he had for his/our future, and he made the adjustments necessary that were favorable to ensure our happiness. While he was making these adjustments, I realized this was a phase that he had to go through, and it allowed me to be patient while he made those adjustments.

This was his experience, but we both had to deal with the process and its consequences. During this time, we both realized that if an experience affects one in the household, it is felt by both, and because we had become one, we had to meander through this process to make us whole.

COMMITMENT: When you enter into a relationship, the first thing that needs to be verbalized is, *Do we want to be committed to each other?* If there is not an affirmative answer from both parties, rushing to the alter would not be advised. Rushing to the altar will not change or fix the mindset one has of commitment. If the relationship is promising, this may be a time to consider some couples counseling.

COMPASSION: Have you ever seen the overly expressive couple who seem to have enough passion for everyone around them? This type of PDA (public display of affection), most of the time, becomes uncomfortable for others. It often makes you wonder, *Is this to convince others that they love each other, or do they really love each other that much?*

Although love is an action word, real love is not to be made a spectacle display. To be clear, passion in a relationship is good. Truth be told, that is what brought many relationships together. However, there is a difference between passion and compassion. Passion is the intense emotion that drives you toward one another, while compassion is the empathy and care you feel for each other. Committed relationships at one time or another will need to have both—passion at times and compassion at other times.

Compassion is an unselfish act of kindness, understanding, and love, but it should never be replaced with passion. In other words, there will be times when your partner needs your compassion, and that is not a time to offer them passion because, if you do, your partner's needs will not be met. For instance, if your partner has been hurt by something in life (loss of a person, loss of a job, or even a failed adventure), it would not be a good time to suggest sex. Your partner now needs your presence, your love, and your understanding of where they are mentally and emotionally in that moment.

Now, we must say how you handle your partner when they need your compassion may lead to sex, but never substitute one for the other. The longer you are with your spouse and the more you cultivate your relationship, the more you will understand and figure out when they need one or the other.

While passion has its place in marriage, compassion is an invaluable asset. There will be times when you will have to see things from your partner's point of view and table what you may be feeling at that time. Having compassion for your partner in different life stages allows patience to develop, and navigating these stages together requires deep empathy, understanding, sensitivity, gentleness, and consideration, especially during the more difficult times, such as coping with the loss of a loved one.

For example, in 2011, I lost my dad. I had experienced death before, but this was almost too close for me to breathe. As I was beginning to get my footing after the death of my dad, my mother died two years later. I was completely devastated. The matriarch and pillar of our family was gone. My husband had to have compassion for me during this process because, at times, my grief had me all over the place. His compassion allowed him to stand by me with patience and understanding, recognizing that my emotions were unpredictable.

Compassion in a marriage is being present and offering support without judgment or expectation, showing unconditional love to your partner.

COMPROMISE: This is a mutual agreement between spouses. It means that each of us has come to a satisfactory resolution. It doesn't mean that one spouse has gotten the upper hand and the other spouse has had to concede. That is how the world bargains, but for us who want our lives to be living examples to others, we want to be able to edify each other and do it where it brings glory to God.

Judges 16 tells the story of Samson and Delilah. Samson was a powerful man chosen by God. He was a judge over all of Israel, but he had a soft spot for a harlot, Delilah. The first compromise he made was choosing someone who was not on the same social level as him. The Bible tells us in 2 Corinthians 6:14 (NIV), "Do not be yoked together with unbelievers. For what do righteousness and wickedness have in common? Or what fellowship can light have with darkness?"

The term "yoked" references the way farmers would put animals that were of the same size and stature together to till the ground. An older faster animal could not till the ground with a younger slower animal. The tilling would be uneven. It is the same way with marriages. When you are "yoked" with someone, you are spiritually tied to that person. You should share the same family values, ethics, beliefs, or morals. If, in a partnership or marriage, you are yoked with someone who doesn't have the same vision or share the same values as you, it will be somewhat difficult to have a successful marriage.

For example, a person who doesn't want children shouldn't be yoked with someone who has dreams of being a parent and having a family. A Christian should not be yoked with a non-believer or atheist. In each of these scenarios, the belief systems and goals are not the same, and these relationships would eventually encounter conflicts within themselves and with each other.

Because Samson was smitten with Delilah, it caused him to have a lapse in judgment, and this caused him to compromise his beliefs and the things he stood for.

THE TERMS OF MARRIAGE

When choosing a life partner, you cannot compromise what you believe. You must go into the relationship transparent about who you are. When Larry and I decided we were ready for marriage, we discussed with each other what marriage would look like for each of us. At that time, I was part of a Gospel Ensemble that rehearsed, traveled, and performed extensively, and I wasn't willing to totally abandon being a part of something I basically grew up doing. As a compromise, Larry and I decided that he would attend many of the events so that we had time together. To this day, that compromise has turned into a great attribute of our relationship. We are now faithful prayer partners, and we are presently doing ministry together.

We also wanted to note that the concept of being equally yoked to a partner does not just involve marriage. It is relevant for any type of partnership. Whether it is a relationship, a friendship, or a business partnership, this same rule should apply.

COUNSELING: Every couple should consider counseling at some time. This could be from someone licensed in the field of marriage, a Clergyman, or your Pastor. Friends and family will tend to give you information based on their biases, whether they like or dislike your partner. Therefore, the intel you receive from them will be biased as well. This is why counseling can give you a fresh perspective on any issues you may be facing in your relationship.

There have been times when we have been able to have some valuable conversations with some of our family members whose marriages have stood the test of time, and these conversations shed light on life lessons and the challenges of different ages and stages of life. However, we advise you to seek counseling for any deep-rooted issues that may arise within yourself and/or your relationships because a counselor can provide lifelong tools to help weed out some of the roots of the problems you may be facing and strengthen the bond between you and your spouse.

FAITHFULNESS: In this day and age, faithfulness is something that has depreciated in value as relationships are being redefined. Nowadays, the traditional arrangement of marriage has metamorphosized into all sorts of situational arrangements. Through the agreements of polygamy, throuples, and every other re-imagined relationship, faithfulness has not only taken on another meaning, but for many, it is irrelevant or it just doesn't exist.

There are many forms of unfaithfulness, and if we are honest with ourselves, we all have had a struggle or two when it comes to being faithful. It can be experienced by a partner stepping out and having some form of physical or sexual relationship. However, emotional infidelity is just as hurtful, and, in many cases, it can be more damaging.

Emotional infidelity is any emotional feelings that are attached to someone outside of your marriage. This includes but is not limited to having secret conversations with someone else, secret meetings or lunch dates with someone, etc.

Infidelity is not just acts that happen with someone outside of your marriage. Any form of lying, cheating, and deceit is being unfaithful. This can also apply to finances, assets and liabilities, business moves, and partnerships. If you have failed to disclose any secret money, accounts, liaisons with other people, hidden decisions, tangible property, etc. to your partner, these things are considered infidelity as well. Address any underlying issues in the relationship quickly, as this often leads to unfaithfulness. Seek the help of a counselor as a moderator if needed.

FORGIVENESS: The scripture teaches us that forgiveness is transactional. Matthew 6:12 tells us that our debts are forgiven as we forgive our debtors. Matthew 6:14-15 (NKJV) says, "For if you forgive men their trespasses, your heavenly Father will also forgive you. But if you do not forgive men their trespasses, neither will your Father forgive your trespasses." The Message Bible says it this way:

"In prayer, there is a connection between what God does and what you do. You can't get forgiveness from God, for instance, without also forgiving others. If you refuse to do your part, you cut yourself off from God's part." I don't know anyone who would willingly exclude themselves from "God's part." That is a powerful explanation of this scripture. When you fail to forgive your spouse, you are out of fellowship with your partner. You are cutting yourself off from all the wonderful things that your partner has to offer you.

We know that forgiveness is important because, in Luke 23:34, that was one of Jesus' last requests of God the Father on the cross. If Jesus took the time before He took His dying breath to ask the Father to forgive the sinners who put him on the cross and those who were hanging on the cross with Him, then surely, we should take forgiveness a little more seriously.

There are two phrases you should be comfortable with besides "You're right" and "I was wrong." They are "I'm sorry" and "Forgive me." So many arguments and misunderstandings would have been cut short if someone simply said those words.

Because unforgiveness can make it difficult to see the real issue, there are times when you must be willing to forgive before there is a resolution to the problem. If you are willing to let go of the unforgiveness and take a minute to see the issue from another viewpoint, you may arrive at a solution sooner than you think. You and your partner will always have your own opinions about certain things, and that's where the differences come in. Both parties should be willing to empathize with the other's frame of reference on forgiveness.

Although we are talking about marriages in this book, many families, friendships, corporations, communities, churches, and other organizations break down and fall out because of unforgiveness. Forgiveness must be a regular tool that you use in any relationship, especially in marriage.

INTIMACY: You cannot have true intimacy without fully trusting your partner. TD Jakes said, "Intimacy means into me see." That statement is so true. There is a closeness in intimacy that is more than the physical act of sex. Intimacy is a place where the touch of heart and spirit is so deep that you never have to physically touch, but the connection is undeniable.

There are several forms of intimacy, and it can be categorized as emotional, physical, and spiritual. Emotional intimacy builds the trust and closeness needed for healthy physical intimacy, while spiritual intimacy can provide a shared sense of purpose and deeper connection. When all three are nurtured, they contribute to a balanced, strong, and enduring relationship between you and your partner.

For example, there are some things that I have felt and experienced that only my spouse knows about me. I have never spoken or shared those experiences with anyone else. That does not disqualify my family and friends from being supportive, but because of the level of intimacy and trust that has been developed in my marriage, we both have the freedom to share our deepest secrets.

Intimacy is also developed through communication. Thinking back on our marriage, we were not afraid to be open, honest, and intimate about everything. We were comfortable sharing with each other and having hard conversations. If we made a mistake, we admitted it. We freely shared our thoughts and feelings with one another and tried our best not to keep secrets. We can honestly say that this level of intimacy helped us become more in sync with each other.

MUTUAL SUBMISSION: As we said earlier, submission is not a bad word, and we understand this topic is a little tricky for some people, both men and women. The modern-day woman thinks that if she submits to her husband, she has no control or say about anything. That is not true. To submit does not mean you are the weaker vessel, and submitting doesn't take away independence or your voice.

Mutual submission is a matter of trust. I, as the wife, trust my husband as the head of the family to lead, guide, and support the family as God leads him to do so. My husband trusts that I, as the wife, will wholeheartedly support the plans as he is led by God. Will the wife have input? Yes! Will the husband, at times, need to confer with his wife? Yes! That's why it is mutual and not just one-sided submission. It takes a submitted man not to cheat on his wife. It takes a submitted man to understand that his wife is to be honored and not disrespected. When a husband submits to Christ and has the love of God in his heart, his wife sees and experiences this kind of submission, so it makes it that much easier for her to submit to her husband.

PARTNERSHIP: When you take the leap into a committed relationship, you must have partnership in mind. There are no solo acts in marriage. It's not "I'm getting a new car." It's "We're getting a new car." It's no longer "I have a new venture." It's "We have a new venture."

In a partnership, whether it is a business partnership or a relationship partnership, everyone attached to the partnership shares in the gains and losses. That's why it's imperative that everyone in the partnership is transparent and does not have secrets. If someone decides to take on a venture by themselves and it fails, then both parties suffer the loss. The same is true if the outcome is a positive one. If someone in the partnership receives an award, reward, or accomplishment, both will share in the gain of the benefit. It makes no sense to be on the same team but play against each other. We are not saying that you lose your individuality, but the end goal is to be on one accord, like-minded, and unified with the same goals and intentions for the partnership.

There is a heavily used phrase that many people quote, and that is "ride or die." This phrase has been mentioned in hip-hop culture and rap music, but it originated in 1950 with motorcycle riders. They would say this because they enjoyed the freedom of riding motorcycles so much that they would rather die if they couldn't ride.

We truly gave the term "ride or die" some grit. We really looked out for each other and protected each other. We didn't let anyone in our family or outside our family talk negatively about the other. We decided early on in our relationship that if we were to survive the test of time, we could not involve other people in our relationship unnecessarily. We were so committed to making things work that we did not allow anyone to disrupt our household. This was a hard thing to do at times. It sometimes meant that we were not always able to share every crisis with our family or friends. The problem with sharing too many of your intimate details in a crisis is that, once the crisis is over, family and friends may still have issues with what happened. The problem is solved for us, but family members and friends are still upset because they have gotten emotionally attached to one of your issues. This is not fair to either spouse.

During a time when we had some financial issues, my husband and I were determined to be responsible and handle the situation on our own. My husband was working for the apartment complex that we lived in when he called me and told me that our lights had been turned off. We knew that his mother or my mother would have done anything to help us out, but we decided that we would "ride" things out because we knew we would be getting paid a day or so later.

Here's where the "ride or die" first came in for us: There was an empty apartment across the breezeway from us that was vacant but had electricity, and my husband did maintenance for the apartments. He went into the vacant apartment, got an extension cord, and ran it from our apartment to the apartment with power so that we could make it through the next couple of days.

We made the best of a bad situation but did not blame each other for our misfortune. We actually had time to reset and check in with each other on a different level because there were no distractions (i.e., no power for the TV or any electronics). Remarkably, today, we still have that "ride or die" attitude with each other and our family.

No one in either of our families knows this story (until now) because that's how determined we were to make things work. We love our families, and neither of us wanted our families to judge the other for this incident. We wanted to respect their place in our lives, and we wanted our families to respect our commitment to each other and to know that we were serious about our partnership.

It may be hard not to reveal every little detail to your mother, father, sister, brother, or others in your family, but revealing all of your hardships to family can sometimes complicate your relationship. Don't do this disservice to your relationship. Trust each other and give each other grace and a chance to grow.

Please note: This method does not apply if there is some sort of abuse taking place in your relationship or home. If there is something of that nature going on, we strongly advise you to get the help you need by speaking to someone you trust or getting professional help.

RESPECT: We are basically taught from the womb the importance of respect and to respect those who have earned a place of respect in our lives. However, respect is something that we will freely give to someone who we admire, honor, esteem, and have high regard and appreciation for. As you build your relationship together, always keep in mind that this is a person you want to respect and have that respect returned back to you. So, everything you do should be intentional in building the level of respect you desire to receive. In other words, don't do anything or say anything to your partner that would cause them to lose respect for you.

Disrespect in any relationship or marriage is like a physical slap in the face, and no one wants to be slapped. It is one of the most degrading things you can do in a relationship. When you disrespect your partner, it not only hurts them but also creates a rift between the two of you. When you have an instance that may lead to actions or words of disrespect, pause and take a minute to think of a physical slap. If you must walk away for a moment, do so and return when you can resume a conversation or interaction that is more positive. This will lead to harmony in your relationship and not hate and resentment.

One way to keep respect in your relationship is to set clear boundaries. Discuss what is okay and not okay. In our marriage, one of our deal breakers is that we are never to call each other out of their name. Today, because of the changes in society, it is quite trendy to call women (and men) all the street names that are being recited in music and on TV. For us, it has never been acceptable in our relationship to do that. We valued the qualities that we saw in each other, and it was very important that we didn't taint our marriage by using negative descriptions of each other. If we attached those negative connotations to each other early on in the relationship, then our responses to each other would have been negative throughout the entire relationship. There were times in our lives when we experienced hardships, and those times were already enough for us to navigate. It would not have been beneficial for either of us to add insult to injury by blaming each other or calling each other names. I found that the more I encouraged my spouse with positive affirmations, the more it yielded positive results in his actions.

Proverbs 23:7a (NKJV) says, "For as he thinks in his heart, so is he." Self-respect is just as important as respect in a relationship. If you have no respect for yourself, you cannot respect others, including your spouse.

TRUST: During the early days of dating, our relationship was so pure and innocent. Those were "puppy love" days—talking on the phone for hours, walking home from high school hand-in-hand, and sharing snacks and conversations as we walked. In the beginning of our relationship, our trust was untainted. However, once trust was broken, trust became a problem.

Larry and I trusted each other until we were given reasons not to extend that trust any longer. When this happens in a relationship, it is usually the time when we are tempted to fact-check each other, check each other's alibis and cellphones, watch each other's expressions for signs of lying—you get the picture. Trust that always needs to be tested in a relationship becomes a continuous interrogation. Then, we get to the stage where we say we trust each other, but we still need to verify. Spoiler alert: That's still not trust.

Complete trust in your partner allows you to go deeper. You will find that your partner knows things about you that you have not verbalized to anyone else. Trust creates a bond so strong that you have confidence in what your partner will and won't do away from your presence, and that is the type of trust that builds a relationship and does not destroy it.

Chapter 4
The Home of Marriage

Have you ever had the opportunity to witness a couple's demeanor after being together for many years? They seem to be able to anticipate each other's needs, complete each other's sentences, and have a knack for making the art of relationships look easy. But if you take the time to talk with these couples, you'll find that it took years of trial and error to get to that point in marriage.

The reason they can make things look like a well-oiled machine is because they endured times of failure, missed cues, miscommunications, and misunderstandings. All of these misfortunes were beneficial for the growth of their relationship. In our personal journey, we have had some of these same experiences and difficulties, but we understand that difficulty in a relationship doesn't mean the destruction of a relationship.

We've all seen or at least are familiar with the movie *The Wizard of Oz*. This movie has several famous quotes that are still recited to this day, such as "There's No Place Like Home." This quote is simple yet powerful in its meaning. Throughout the movie, it was repeated to drive home the yearning desire of the fictional character, Dorothy, to return home. Her ultimate goal was to return to the place where she felt safe, secure, and comfortable.[1]

If we are honest, home, for many people, is not a desired place to be. Home, for some, is a place of dysfunction and conflict. In marriage, this should not be the goal. When we create our homes, our goal should be to create our safe space, our comfort zone, our refuge, our place of peace and tranquility. When we view marriage, we should have the same idea. What we feel about creating a home should be interchangeable with what we feel about building a marriage. The concepts are essentially the same. We expect our marriages to be a desired place, just like home, and our homes and our marriages should never be a place of dread.

I know you might be thinking, *This is not how I have observed marriages in this day and time.* Yes, you are right, to a degree. The commitment of marriage that we are referring to is according to the biblical standard of marriage, not as the world has designed it to be.

Here's what the Bible says concerning marriage:

"Therefore shall a man leave his father and his mother and shall cleave unto his wife: and they shall be one flesh."
~Genesis 2:24 (KJV)

The phrase "cleave" in this context is the act of severing one tie to clinging to another one. In this case, the man is severing the tie with his biological family to create his own tie with his wife and family.

"And he answered and said unto them, Have ye not read, that he which made them at the beginning made them male and female, And said, For this cause shall a man leave father and mother, and shall cleave to his wife: and they twain shall be one flesh? Wherefore they are no more twain, but one flesh. What therefore God hath joined together, let not man put asunder." ~Matthew 19:4-6 (KJV)

THE HOME OF MARRIAGE

The word "asunder" means to divide, to pull apart, or to break into bits and pieces. The "asunder" things (the things causing division) are considered the outside elements, the bits and pieces that keep a marriage from thriving. Outside elements are not just the things and circumstances that disrupt, distract, and attempt to destroy a marriage; this also includes outside people. Outside people are those who do not have the well-being of your relationship at heart. These people should be treated as an outside element and a threat to your relationship. Their sole mission is to present negativity, doubt, and confusion, and the inclusion of outside people could ultimately be the demise of what could be a flourishing relationship.

Please note that not all outside people are there to damage your relationship. There will be those who have the best interest of your relationship at heart, and you will, with time, know who can be trusted in your inner circle of marriage.

Marriage should be a place of shelter, a place of covering—the place that guarantees us protection from outside influences and pressures. To do this, there are several inside elements that a marriage should contain. These include communication, compassion, compromise, commitment, faithfulness, trust, intimacy, acceptance, respect, partnership, mutual submission, and forgiveness (for more information, see "Terms of Marriage" chapter).

Let's take communication for example: Communication is a tough subject for marriages. One of the top reasons for divorce is communication problems. Oftentimes, when we hear the word "communication," we automatically think of confrontation. We think there's a problem. Consider this: How can you create a safe, happy space if you don't talk with each other? How can you meet your collective goals or be effective for each other in the marriage if you expect each other to just know or figure it out?

Men and women tend to be opposite in their thought processes. Because we are made differently, we communicate differently. What a husband considers a clean house is totally different from what a wife would consider a clean house. What the husband has in mind when he decides to clean the house may take thirty minutes, but when the wife does it, it may take all day.

Just as with communication, you can apply this same thought process to any area of married life. This could be applied to your children, finances, assets, goals, etc. In any of these areas, you may get two different answers based on which perspective or response you are seeking. That's why it's imperative that each person in the marriage verbalize their expectations before and during marriage.

The Home of Marriage Reflections

What is your definition of "home"?

THE HOME OF MARRIAGE

Does your ideal home environment match your reality? Why or why not?

What does a healthy marriage look like to you?

THE HOME OF MARRIAGE

Have you created a safe place (free of outside elements) for your marriage to thrive? If so, how? If not, what steps can you take to protect your home from outside elements?

_____
_____
_____
_____
_____
_____
_____
_____
_____
_____
_____
_____
_____
_____
_____
_____
_____
_____
_____
_____
_____
_____
_____
_____
_____
_____
_____
_____
_____

THE HOME OF MARRIAGE

What did you find helpful in "The Home of Marriage" chapter for you and your relationship?

List one thing from this chapter that you can incorporate in your relationship moving forward.

Chapter 5
The Yard

The yard of a home is the crown jewel. It's what gives the home the curb appeal and can be the deciding factor for many people when buying a home. The yard is the home's first impression, and as a homeowner, you want to make sure that everything is in its place and that it's aesthetically pleasing to the eye of those who pass by. However, although things are nicely trimmed, edged, and nicely manicured, there are times when what's in the yard doesn't match what's on the inside. You may get a peek inside the door and realize that the entire house is in disarray. The yard can be deceiving as to what's really going on inside. Relationships can be the same way.

Have you ever seen those couples that look like they have it all together? Everything is in sync. They dress alike and finish each other's sentences, yet a few years later, they are divorced. Their relationship was a metaphorically impeccable yard. Their efforts went into convincing others that the relationship was more solid than it appeared, and they spent a lot of time and effort on the landscape but neglected the interior of the relationship.

There are times when the yard needs regular maintenance and upkeep. This requires mowing the grass, pulling up weeds, pruning trees and shrubs, and watering and preparing flower beds for upcoming seasons. Your relationship will require periodic maintenance as well. You will encounter times when you need to check in with your partner to see where they are mentally and emotionally.

To get to the root of issues in a relationship, you often have to dig deep into past issues to resolve the present ones. For example, we came across a couple who was having intimacy issues in their relationship. After several instances of making their partner feel rejected, they began to open up about a trauma that happened in the past. This allowed their spouse to get an inside view of what was happening, and it released them to have the freedom they needed for intimacy.

Hidden trauma of any kind, whether physical, mental, sexual, or emotional, can cause irreparable damage to a relationship if ignored. These are the things you definitely want to prune away through regular maintenance. Some trauma is too deep to handle alone. If this is the case, it is imperative that you seek professional help.

Years ago, my husband and I went through a season that revealed the importance of digging out the roots of the past. When I was born, I was my mother and father's first child. I was also the first grandchild of my maternal grandparents. Needless to say, I got a lot of attention as a child. Yet, there was one person's attention I yearned for, and that was my dad. He was a military man who had a rigid way of doing things. There was no coloring outside the lines, and everything was black and white. There was definitely no saying I love you, no hugs and kisses, and no showing any type of affection. At the time, I didn't realize this was something that I would carry for years.

As I got older, this really affected my self-esteem and my confidence, and as my husband and I were dating and early in our marriage, I put a lot of pressure on him to show me love and prove that he really loved me. Because I really never received this type of treatment from the one person who was supposed to demonstrate it to me (my dad), I didn't know what to look for. I didn't have a healthy sense of love and affection from the first man in my life, so how could I expect it from the man of my dreams? When this issue was self-identified during a heated conversation between me and my husband, it hit me like a ton of bricks.

Through it all, we were able to work through this challenging time in our relationship because we were not afraid to address the issue by digging deep, pruning, and cutting away any of the behaviors that were not beneficial for our forward progress. I am thankful that my husband was able to look beyond the emotional weeds that started to grow and help me do the work to eliminate the things that would have unearthed the foundation of our home.

In order to survive the stresses that come with marriage, you cannot just maintain a "put together" outer appearance. Your inside (core) needs to be strengthened. There will be many outside elements you face as a couple, and at the core of what you are building, there must be a foundation of trust and reliability that cannot be shaken. There will be individuals that test your relationship, both inside and outside your family, as well as everyday living and life circumstances beyond your control. You must both be on the same page and stand united against any outside elements.

THE HOME OF MARRIAGE

The Yard Reflections

What are some things you can trim away to improve your relationship?

THE YARD

What are some outside elements that may pose a potential threat?

How have you handled the potential threats that have interfered with your relationship?

Is there anything that you could do better next time you encounter these outside elements?

_____
_____
_____
_____
_____
_____
_____
_____
_____
_____
_____
_____
_____
_____
_____
_____
_____
_____
_____
_____
_____
_____
_____
_____
_____
_____
_____
_____
_____

What are some of the traumas that have hindered your relationship from growing, and how are you addressing the issues?

THE YARD

What things have been beneficial to you as it relates to the "yard" of your relationship?

_____
_____
_____
_____
_____
_____
_____
_____
_____
_____
_____
_____
_____
_____
_____
_____
_____
_____
_____
_____
_____
_____
_____
_____
_____
_____
_____
_____

THE HOME OF MARRIAGE

List one thing from this chapter that you can incorporate in your relationship moving forward.

Chapter 6

The Garage, The Attic, and The Basement

The garage, the attic, and the basement are areas of the house where household items may become hidden, stored for later use, or forgotten. When we started talking about writing this book, we had several instances where we wanted to omit certain issues because they were too personal in our eyes. These were the issues we had hidden in the garage, the attic, and the basement of our relationship, and writing this chapter caused us to revisit some of our forgotten areas—the areas where a lot of healing and forgiveness had to take place and trust had to be rebuilt. Ultimately, we agreed that if this book was to truly be beneficial to other couples, we had to include the hard, honest truth.

There may be hidden issues or stored-up feelings from your past. These may be events that happened in your life that you thought you were released from until, one day, you were triggered. It may also be past relationships or present issues in your relationship that hinder your forward progress. These things are important to discuss and deal with as soon as they are recognized.

Hiding your feelings and your views on situations does not resolve conflict. Whether the events are pre-existing or current, they will still affect the relationship if you are not open and honest.

Notice we said honest, not hurtful. There is always a way to say what you have to say to your partner without wounding them. If you find that you have difficulty choosing your words wisely in a heightened situation, give each other the time and space to reset so that you can gather your thoughts and feelings without causing a rift in your relationship.

When hidden issues are ignored, it creates roadblocks in your relationship. One of the roadblocks we encountered early in our marriage was a lack of communication when it came to finances. We were both independent when we got together, and it affected our ability to openly share where we were financially. We were both used to taking our income and doing what we thought was necessary to have a functional household, but we failed to communicate clearly what we were doing with each other.

This lack of communication came to a head when we found ourselves in a financially tight situation. Because we did not reveal to each other where we truly were financially, this caused us to face extreme hardship, and we found ourselves in a place of bankruptcy and foreclosure. Although we were able to restore ourselves to a better place, we realized that if we had communicated better up front about the state of our affairs, we could have possibly avoided this hurdle.

The joining of two worlds will inevitably bring together different viewpoints about life events. This can also create openings for masking or stuffing what one really feels in certain situations. Masked and disguised reactions don't allow you to get to the heart of matters.

Years ago, we were faced with one of the saddest times in our lives as we were awaiting the arrival of a new baby. We were discussing names and preparing to paint the room we selected to be the nursery. We never got to that point of our journey because, at five months, the baby was miscarried. My husband and I were devastated, but because we masked our feelings from each other, it took a long time for us to adequately deal with our loss. We hid

THE GARAGE, THE ATTIC, AND THE BASEMENT

our feelings in the garage, the attic, and the basement and tried to go on with life as usual.

This painful moment in our lives caused us to deflect, but when we delayed facing what was hidden, it delayed us from being able to talk honestly about what each of us was feeling so we could get to the point of our healing. Through times like this, we found that facing many of these hidden and concealed areas in our lives has created a stronger, deeper bond between us.

Don't be afraid to face clutter in any area of your relationship. Do the spring cleaning necessary to clear out the obstructions in your relationship that restrict growth and harmony. The realization of things that have been stuffed away does not always result in a negative outcome. Unmasking and revealing hidden stuff can help you understand your partner better and give you insight into how you can help each other.

Please Note: If these hidden issues include deeper issues, such as cheating or extramarital affairs that may or may not include outside children, we highly suggest the involvement of a licensed professional for further assistance. Do not attempt something of this magnitude without the intervention of a professional.

The Garage the Attic and the Basement Reflections

Is there anything hidden that keeps you from being transparent with your partner (i.e., past abuse of any kind, abandonment issues, etc.)?

THE GARAGE, THE ATTIC, AND THE BASEMENT

Has there been any infidelity (physical, emotional, or financial) that has happened that has not been addressed or fully forgiven?

Are there any areas in your relationship where you may be harboring hidden or suppressed emotions?

THE GARAGE, THE ATTIC, AND THE BASEMENT

Do you feel your partner is harboring any hidden or suppressed emotions? Why or why not?

THE HOME OF MARRIAGE

List one thing from this chapter that you can incorporate in your relationship moving forward.

Chapter 7
The Living Room

The living room of a home is where you kick back and relax after a hard day of work. It is where you may sit around and watch television or catch up with your loved ones. It is also the room where most of the family's entertainment takes place. In some families, this room is called the front room or the den. Nevertheless, living rooms are usually a place of comfort and community and usually where the family gathers for all occasions.

Have you ever noticed that when something happens in a marriage, there are more people affected than the two in the marriage? When a couple faces a separation or divorce, the family and friends around them also deal with the hardship. It really does take a village to build a family, and it takes the support of family and friends to help navigate times of adversity. That's why it is of the essence that the couple is sure about embarking on the journey of marriage.

On your journey of marriage, you must make sure that you have times when you are able to relax, reset, and catch up with your partner. This secures the bond between you and your spouse. You must take time to step away from talking about to-do lists, bills, deadlines, what's going on with the kids (usually a lot), and other family issues to relax and enjoy the comfort of each other. When you are deliberate about the health of your relationship, everyone in the heart of the home benefits.

The funny thing about living areas that stood out for us back in our day was the way we had a formal living room and a den. At our granny's house, the formal living room had plastic chair covers and carpet runners to protect the fancy furniture and shag carpet. This room was off limits, especially to the kids, and you would be threatened within an inch of your life if you brought any food or drinks in there. This space was only for those select visitors who would come by on occasion but were not staying very long.

Our den was a little more laid back. We could bring in snacks, and there were not as many rules to follow. This is how certain areas of your relationship with your spouse will be. There will be areas in your relationship that should be off-limits to everyone except you and your partner, and, on the other hand, there will be areas that you will need to allow others in to get clarity on minor issues or to help settle differences in opinion. But please keep in mind that whoever you allow to be a mediator cannot be biased and must have a good view of what a healthy relationship is supposed to look like. This would include a couple who has been happily and successfully married, as well as your Pastor, Clergyman, or Clergywoman. Because everyone in the living room (your family) will be affected by any dysfunction that arises, it is vitally important that you build a place of comfort and community not only with those who are in the household but also among friends and family.

The Living Room Reflections

What are some things you can do as a couple to make the space of your relationship more enjoyable and not task-driven?

_____

What activities can you do as a couple that will encourage keeping things light-hearted in a stressful environment?

THE LIVING ROOM

Ask each other this question: What activity would you like us to do to make sure we stay connected emotionally and reset when things get stressful? Note each other's response below:

_____
_____
_____
_____
_____
_____
_____
_____
_____
_____
_____
_____
_____
_____
_____
_____
_____
_____
_____
_____
_____
_____
_____
_____
_____
_____
_____
_____
_____

What are some things you can do as individuals in a relationship to ensure your partner has a safe space?

How can a healthy relationship be beneficial to those around you who observe it?

List one thing from this chapter that you can incorporate in your relationship moving forward.

Chapter 8
The Kitchen

There is nothing more irritating than going to the kitchen to prepare your favorite meal or snack and realizing you don't have all the ingredients you need to prepare it. The same applies to marriage. As you prepare for marriage, you need the right ingredients to honor the commitment. Too many of us have started marriages with too few ingredients, the wrong ingredients, or no ingredients at all. In any case, a marriage cannot survive with insufficient ingredients, incorrect ingredients, or the absence of ingredients.

What are the needed ingredients for a successful marriage? The main ingredient you need is commitment. If your mind is not set to ride the wings of marriage through every life circumstance, that will become the demise of what could be a lasting union.

The other ingredients mentioned at the beginning of this book (see "Terms of Marriage" section) were communication, compromise, intimacy, acceptance, respect, partnership, and mutual submission. All of these ingredients are needed for a good, healthy, solid relationship.

My maternal grandmother was an excellent cook. As a child, I watched her make fresh biscuits for my grandpa every day for many years. I was so intrigued by her skill in making these biscuits so perfectly every time. They would still be piping hot from the oven as soon as my grandpa got home from work.

When my husband and I got married, I had the bright idea that I would try to make biscuits like my grandmother. *How hard could it be?* I had watched her for years as she made these biscuits that everyone in our family coveted. This was all before the times of diehard vegans and gluten-free foods.

I got the ingredients and prepared to try my culinary hand at these victuals. But before I started the task, I figured, let me just call my grandmother in a last-minute, good-faith gesture to ensure my baking success. Once I made sure I had all the ingredients and the correct measurements, all I needed was some instructions.

My grandmother kept telling me to "add all your ingredients in, but don't overwork your dough." I couldn't understand why she was making such a fuss about this part. I think I may have heard her say ten times during our conversation, "Don't overwork the dough."

I later found out that if the dough is overworked, the biscuits will not come out right. My biscuits were okay while they were hot, but as soon as they cooled down, they were as hard as hockey pucks. My husband and son thought this was hilarious and got a few laughs at my expense. I learned the hard way that you should mix the dough just enough to combine all the ingredients.

I told this story because many times in our relationships, we have all the right ingredients for a successful relationship or marriage, but we don't always follow the instructions that will keep us from "overworking" the strength of our relationship.

Being overworked is any type of behavior that takes your spouse for granted. Being overworked is leaving your partner out on an island by themselves and not sharing the burden or responsibility that comes with upholding a household, a family, and your relationship all at the same time. Being overworked also is drawing a line in the sand and saying, *This is the wife's responsibility, or this is the husband's responsibility.* There will be times along the way when the wife may

THE KITCHEN

have to help her husband by taking out the trash. In turn, the husband may have to wash a dish or maybe even cook, especially when both work outside the home.

We are in no way trying to minimize anyone's role or responsibilities. We have experienced this several times during our journey when one of us had major surgery or a medical procedure, and we were not able to do any of our regular tasks, sometimes for weeks. But because of our partnership agreement, we never missed a beat in getting things done.

I'm so committed to being in partnership with my husband that I have my own toolbox, literally. I wouldn't dare wait until my husband got home from a hard day's work to ask him to handle something broken that I'd looked at all day and could have fixed. That's not being very considerate. So, I'm not beyond taking out the trash and changing light bulbs and filters. You must have this sort of attitude and determination. *What if something happened physically to your partner, and there's not an option to hire someone for every little thing?* There should be an understanding that we are both headed to the same destination, and to get there, it will take teamwork.

Another area where the relationship can become overworked is in finances. Don't assume, because you may be the highest breadwinner in the home, that what you say goes and that's final. As husband and wife, you should always share in whatever decisions are made. Both share the responsibility and outcome, so both should have a say and be able to input their views on what affects you.

There will be times when you get to different ages and stages in life where the wife may be the primary source of income. Then, at other times, the husband may be the primary source of income. But when you remember that you are in a covenant partnership with your spouse, there is no primary or secondary income. It is all brought to one table for a common goal, and that is to build a solid foundation in your home and family.

In 1978, Teddy Pendergrass released a song entitled "When Somebody Loves You Back." One of the lines in the song talks about love as a percentage and how we're not supposed to have a 70-30 or a 60-40, but we should have 50-50 love.[2] My husband and I disagree with Teddy regarding all these percentages. After decades of marriage, we understand that we have been successful in marriage because we both have been all in at 100 percent. If I am only giving 50 percent participation, where is my other 50 percent going? We both have to be at max performance if we are to successfully make it through this life of marriage together.

THE KITCHEN

The Kitchen Reflections

What ingredients do I feel that I am lacking the most when it comes to my relationship? Commitment, communication, compromise, intimacy, acceptance, respect, partnership, and mutual submission.

_____
_____
_____
_____
_____
_____
_____
_____
_____
_____
_____
_____
_____
_____
_____
_____
_____
_____
_____
_____
_____
_____
_____
_____
_____

How can I improve in these area(s)?

THE KITCHEN

Are there areas where I feel like I have been overworked (taken for granted) in? Why or why not?

_____
_____
_____
_____
_____
_____
_____
_____
_____
_____
_____
_____
_____
_____
_____
_____
_____
_____
_____
_____
_____
_____
_____
_____
_____
_____
_____
_____

Ask your partner if there are any areas that they feel they have been taken for granted in as well? Why do they feel this way?

___

THE KITCHEN

As you explore your partner's point of view, describe below, in your own words, what your partner is trying to convey to you:

_____
_____
_____
_____
_____
_____
_____
_____
_____
_____
_____
_____
_____
_____
_____
_____
_____
_____
_____
_____
_____
_____
_____
_____
_____
_____
_____
_____

What are some things that you and your partner can do to ensure your partner does not feel overworked or taken for granted in the future?

_____
_____
_____
_____
_____
_____
_____
_____
_____
_____
_____
_____
_____
_____
_____
_____
_____
_____
_____
_____
_____
_____
_____
_____
_____

THE KITCHEN

Are there areas of responsibility that we can share or switch up to ease the burden on the other in times of crisis or crunch?

What are some things you can add (ingredients) to make sure things stay fresh and spicy in your relationship?

_____
_____
_____
_____
_____
_____
_____
_____
_____
_____
_____
_____
_____
_____
_____
_____
_____
_____
_____
_____
_____
_____
_____
_____
_____
_____
_____
_____
_____

THE KITCHEN

When you think of your future with your spouse:

Can you see yourself growing old with them? **Yes or No.**

Can you see yourself being a caretaker for this person if something unexpected happens in life? **Yes or No.**

Can you see yourself happy with this person in whatever age and stage of life you are in? **Yes or No.**

If you answered yes, describe what feelings came up as you considered these questions. If you answered no, take some time to reflect on your motivations for remaining in the relationship and describe them below.

_____
_____
_____
_____
_____
_____
_____
_____
_____
_____
_____
_____
_____
_____
_____
_____
_____
_____

Chapter 9
The Bedroom

We have mentioned in other parts of this book that the home is a place of comfort and rest, and a happy, healthy marriage should mirror this idea. The bedroom is the place where comfort, rest, and relaxation should take place. Many of us have made our bedrooms places that are not conducive to positive benefits. They have become gyms, home offices, and extended baby nurseries.

The bedroom should be one of the more private areas. It should be the inner sanctum of the home. The bedroom is where many of the characteristics we spoke about earlier (intimacy, communication, trust, etc.) will be tested. There are moments that happen in the bedroom that shouldn't be shared with anyone else but your partner.

Hebrews 13:4 (KJV) says, "Marriage is honourable in all, and the bed undefiled." That word "undefiled" simply means pure. In the sanctity of marriage, what goes on behind the closed doors of your bedroom is pure.

We always have a chuckle here because it mimics the slogan that was created for tourists going to Las Vegas: *"What happens here, stays here."* The Las Vegas Convention and Visitors Authority, along with their advertising partners, wanted those who came to their city to have the freedom of enjoying themselves without judgment.[3] This is applicable in the personal space of your bedrooms as well. The bedroom should be special for you and your partner. You should be able to express whatever your heart desires in the space of your bedroom without the judgment of your spouse, and what goes on should not be discussed or shared with anyone outside of your marriage. There shouldn't be anyone advising you on what goes on in this personal space.

Have you ever felt protective and guarded when someone other than your spouse wants to come into your bedroom? That's because the bedroom is an area where you feel the most vulnerable and probably the place where you have had to face a lot of personal, emotional, and spiritual truths.

As we previously mentioned, the bedroom is the inner sanctum for you and your partner. It is a private, intimate, and sacred space where you and your spouse can relax, connect, and enjoy personal intimacy away from the outside world. It is also a place to be rejuvenated and revived spiritually.

We also want to caution you: DO NOT LET OTHERS IN YOUR BED! This may sound a little extreme to some, but we advise that you make it a practice not to bring anyone else into your bed. This can apply both mentally and physically. Your bed is a deeply personal space for you and your partner. So, don't allow anyone to invade your sacred space.

Is your bedroom considered a multi-media room? If so, change this immediately. Your bedroom should be a haven for you and your partner to relax, refresh, and reset. It should not be a place of distraction.

It is also important not to have certain discussions in your bedroom. If you want this space to be a place of peace, love, harmony, and resetting, you can't have conversations contrary to the atmosphere you want to set. If your bedroom is a place where you and your spouse continuously have heated discussions (such as bills, family issues, work tasks, etc.) when it comes time for intimacy, you will be triggered by the atmosphere of contention between the two of you. Your bedroom shouldn't be a place of stress and frustration. It should be a place of love and connection.

On the subject of past infidelity, you must make sure that you have dealt with those situations thoroughly as well. You don't want your bedroom to be a reminder of those painful events. If you do not adequately deal with past infidelity, every time there's an encounter in the bedroom, this may trigger past hurt. If this is the case, we suggest getting some professional help to get you through the process.

The Bedroom Reflections

Are you at complete rest and freedom in the retreat of your bedroom? Why or why not?

THE BEDROOM

Have a discussion with your partner about the atmosphere in your bedroom. Note any ideas or suggestions on how you can improve this area of your Home of Marriage.

THE HOME OF MARRIAGE

What steps can you take to make sure no individuals are taking up space in your bedroom (mentally, physically, or emotionally)?

_____
_____
_____
_____
_____
_____
_____
_____
_____
_____
_____
_____
_____
_____
_____
_____
_____
_____
_____
_____
_____
_____
_____
_____
_____
_____

THE BEDROOM

What are some past mistakes/issues (like mistrust or infidelity) that restrict you from being vulnerable with your spouse in your bedroom?

What can you do to break down these barriers to vulnerability?

THE BEDROOM

List one thing from this chapter that you can incorporate in your relationship moving forward.

Chapter 10
The Nursery

The nursery is the place where a husband and wife look to the future. It is a place filled with the hopes and dreams of parenthood, a place filled with a future of possibilities for the little life that will, one day, occupy the space, transforming it into their own playground and sanctuary, where they will grow, explore, and thrive.

The nursery, just like your relationship, represents your common ground. The nursery is where you and your spouse will come together and make decisions that will be beneficial for your marriage and your child. Many couples struggle with where the child sleeps, how old is too old for a child to sleep in your bed, or if they are welcome in your bed at all. These are just a few things that couples cannot agree on.

When you are building healthy relationships as a couple and as parents, you must come to an agreement that is healthy for both of you as a couple and as parents. That idea is different in each case, and it is up to you to come up with a healthy median. It may take a little trial and error, but you will learn what works and does not work. Whatever you decide, just make sure you are consistent with it so it doesn't cause inconsistencies in what you or your child experiences.

An example is letting the child sleep in bed with you. One parent may want the child to sleep in the bed, but the other parent is totally against it. It is usually a good rule of thumb to create these boundaries ahead of time when it comes to issues like this to ensure that it is not something you have conflict over later.

We recognized early on that the same teamwork it took for us to navigate through other areas of our lives was the same teamwork it would take to plan a nursery and ultimately raise a child. Many times, a husband and wife will come together on things like nursery décor and colors, but when it comes to actually raising a child or disciplining a child, their ideas are different. This area has often been a source of contention for many couples. That is why it is important to establish a good foundation of unity. If you are not careful, these areas can be the unfolding of your intimacy and connectedness as a couple.

You must remember that although you are both parents, you were a couple first, and you still have to nurture both relationships. Many couples abandon the relationship because they don't know how to nurture both responsibilities in a healthy way. You cannot abandon either of your roles and responsibilities within these relationships.

One of the best practices for couples is to call out or challenge your partner (in a respectful way) if you feel they are becoming unbalanced in their responsibilities as a parent. When all of your energy is focused on being a parent only and not a partner, it is not unreasonable to hold your spouse accountable for their actions. However, it must be addressed in a loving way that does not disqualify your efforts to be a good parent. This will help keep resentment from building up in the relationship and will help maintain a steady flow of communication.

The first time my husband and I began planning a nursery, we were extremely excited to design a space that would be a safe haven for our baby girl or boy. We were both enthusiastic about paint swatches, nursery furniture, and room décor. The nursery was where we saw our ideas coming together for our bundle of joy.

The nursery was a place of enjoyment and excitement, but it was also a place where we were met with uncertainty, fear, and anxiety.

THE NURSERY

What if we are not good parents? What if we don't know how to care for a baby? We were not alone. These are fears that most new parents face, and there is nothing wrong with feeling this type of anxiety.

When we were planning and creating our nursery, we were faced with a devastating situation. About five months into all the excitement, we experienced a miscarriage. All the hopes, dreams, and plans came to a sudden halt, and we were forced to change our plans for the future we were building. Our focus turned from the expectation of a little one to finding a way to heal from this devastation. On July 15, 1987, we were blessed with a son, Mario, which allowed us to experience and embrace the beauty of transformation that the nursery brings into a marriage.

The Nursery Reflections:

What are the biggest challenges you anticipate (or have experienced) in your parenting journey?

How can you balance your individual needs with the demands of being a parent?

How can you and your partner stay connected and support each other when parenting becomes overwhelming?

What are some strategies you can use to maintain a positive mindset during difficult parenting moments?

How can you handle disagreements about parenting styles or decisions with your spouse?

THE NURSERY

Sit with your spouse and discuss one parenting strategy that you can come to an agreement on before the issue comes up in your marriage. This can include topics such as where your child will sleep, assigning chores, your style of discipline, or another important topic that came to mind. Note the plan below and how it will be implemented when necessary.

_____
_____
_____
_____
_____
_____
_____
_____
_____
_____
_____
_____
_____
_____
_____
_____
_____
_____
_____
_____
_____
_____
_____
_____

List one thing from this chapter that you can incorporate in your relationship moving forward.

_____
_____
_____
_____
_____
_____
_____
_____
_____
_____
_____
_____
_____
_____
_____
_____
_____
_____
_____
_____
_____
_____
_____
_____
_____
_____
_____

Chapter 11
The Empty Nest

The empty nest occurs when the children in the household have grown up and have left home to begin their own independent lives. Unfortunately for us, we experienced an empty nest way earlier than we anticipated. Our empty nest happened because of an inadvertent experience when we were faced with the unexpected loss of a baby. We were not ready or equipped at the time to handle this involuntary misfortune. Needless to say, we both had to learn how to navigate through the feelings of loss, pain, and confusion.

One thing we both discovered during this time is that you cannot run away from whatever emotional roller coaster you may find yourself on. You should both allow a safe space for each other to feel every emotion that arises.

We made a few mistakes during this time by trying to endure our feelings independently. This led to miscommunication and hurt feelings. It is okay to deal with whatever feelings you have about the loss separately, but at some point, you should discuss your feelings with each other. There is a good chance that you are both experiencing the same feelings of distress but are responding to it differently. This is why it is imperative that you and your spouse support one another no matter how intense their feelings are.

Many couples will experience some of the same feelings we felt when faced with their grown children leaving the nest. For the first time, you, as a couple, will face an empty to-do list, empty schedules, and not many events because much of what you did was centered around your children's activities. Although this seems disheartening at first, it is an excellent opportunity to continue building on your relationship and discovering some of the things you and your spouse put on hold while raising a family.

Regrettably, we have seen couples that can't seem to make it work after the children are grown and gone. This can be because they have failed to maintain their spark while raising their children. Our suggestion would be to rediscover the things that made you a couple in the first place. Start planning dates and adventures that help to rebuild what you had before you started to build a family. Go on dates. Make a couple's bucket list. Do something out of your comfort zone.

If you have trouble deciding, explore some of the recommendations in the "Date Night Suggestions" section of this book.

Empty Nest Reflections

What are some of the challenges and/or anxieties you face when considering your empty nest?

_____
_____
_____
_____
_____
_____
_____
_____
_____
_____
_____
_____
_____
_____
_____
_____
_____
_____
_____
_____
_____
_____
_____
_____
_____
_____
_____
_____
_____

How can you overcome some of these challenges?

THE EMPTY NEST

How can you support each other when dealing with the emotions of an empty nest?

What are the adventures you and your spouse can explore?

THE EMPTY NEST

Do you view the empty nest as a challenge or a welcomed adventure? Explain.

List one thing from this chapter that you can incorporate in your relationship moving forward.

Chapter 12

The Junk Drawer

In September of 2022, our son, Mario, got married, and we were blessed with a daughter-in-law, Ebony, who we affectionately call our daughter. We often have heart-to-heart conversations about life, family, and marriage. One day, during one of our times of bonding, our daughter said, "I don't ever want issues in my marriage to become mounds of dirt under the carpet." Her statement sparked my attention mid-conversation, which caused me to examine her statement further.

Mounds of dirt under the carpet are issues that are not addressed between a husband and wife. They are unresolved issues that couples take for granted and expect to go away if ignored long enough.

Another example of this is the junk drawer. Every house has at least one. Yours may be in the kitchen, the bathroom, the bedroom, or the garage, but the reality is some homes have more than one junk drawer.

The junk drawer is where we place everything we want to be hidden from plain sight, including things like extra tools, restaurant condiments and napkins, or random knickknacks. It may also include unknown parts and pieces of things we have found lying around that we keep just in case we figure out where they belong. These drawers are the place where we stick all the little stuff we are hiding—the stuff that we don't want to deal with "right now." Our junk drawers are where we conceal all the miscellaneous stuff that we don't want others to see. Needless to say, our junk drawers are a mess.

As it relates to marriage, each relationship is different, so the contents of your marital junk drawer may differ. These can include all the things that have occurred during the relationship that you have failed to deal with, including dishonesty, infidelity, or a difference in goals, opinions, or vision. These things can fester into anger, resentment, misunderstanding, and lack of communication. The issues that accumulate in the junk drawer need to be dealt with immediately. If you don't face the issues gathering in your relationship's junk drawer, this can become detrimental to your relationship or marriage.

Whether you have mounds of dirt under the carpet or an accumulating junk drawer in your relationship, the bottom line is both need to be addressed with the utmost care. These scenarios could have harmful effects on your relationship if they are ignored. Marriage brings two worlds together, and when there are unresolved issues, those issues will appear at some point, no matter how hard you try to hide them.

Junk Drawer Reflections

Describe any pre-existing issues that could be considered "mounds of dirt"?

What issues have you discovered that may become mounds of dirt if they are not dealt with efficiently in your relationship?

Do either of you have trouble addressing unresolved issues? Why or why not?

What can you do as a couple to sort through some of the issues that are nagging your relationship?

THE JUNK DRAWER

What steps can you agree to now to address future issues immediately so they are not added to the imaginary junk drawer?

THE HOME OF MARRIAGE

List one thing from this chapter that you can incorporate in your relationship moving forward.

Chapter 13
The Doghouse

In many homes around the world, families have pets that are considered family members. Although many see their pets as a part of the family, being a family pet is not a coveted position or category. Likewise, the doghouse is a place where no one in the relationship wants to be, and please note that the doghouse is not a part of the house plan.

Contrary to what most people believe, the doghouse is not gender specific. Most will believe that only men in the relationship do things that confine them to the doghouse, but women can be "sent to the doghouse" as well.

Early on in our marriage, I did things as a husband that should have put me in the doghouse quite often. I found it difficult, at times, to communicate with my wife and did a lot of things without explanation or communication, which offended my wife. Over time, I learned that this is a common mistake with men, although some women do it too. This is one of the biggest reasons a person in a relationship ends up in the doghouse.

For example, when I was still in the hanging out phase, my wife and I talked about never going long periods of time without checking in with each other. But because I was having a great time with my friends, I would stay out later than expected or avoid communicating until I finally made it home. This not only infuriated her, but it also inflated a situation that could have been resolved with a phone call. This one misstep then snowballed into my wife dealing with trust issues and feeling like I had something to hide, thus causing a rift between us.

Through this, I learned that communication is the key to staying out of the doghouse. Ask your partner what are non-negotiables or triggers for them and avoid whatever it is at all costs to preserve the peace and unity in your home.

Admittedly, my issue was that I did not communicate enough. However, my wife's issue was the complete opposite. She would over-communicate, and her wordy dialogue would often wound my spirit. In the heat of the moment, her words were often misunderstood, or they wouldn't come out the way she intended, and this would put her in the doghouse with me.

When we tell our partners that they will be put in the doghouse, this is not a term of endearment. It is a term that lets them know that we are displeased with their actions, whether it was in thought, word, or deed. This reference lets your partner know that you are not on the same page at the moment, that you are not seeing things the same way, and, in many cases, that you are not happy about the current state of your relationship.

According to Google, the term "the doghouse" derived from a 1926 glossary of criminal language and behavior. It defines the doghouse as being in "disfavor." The doghouse has negative connotations and refers to anyone who has not conducted themselves as worthy to be in the company of others or be a part of the harmony in the home.

If your goal is to have a successful marriage and live in peace and harmony, being in "disfavor" with your partner is not beneficial to the health or success of your marriage or relationship. We do not want to find ourselves "in the doghouse" or "in disfavor" with our spouse. We do not want to be in the same category as the family's pet.

THE JUNK DRAWER

To make sure we do not cause irreparable damage in our marriages and relationships, the doghouse should not be an option. That's why we make a point to say the doghouse is not a part of the house plan—it should not be a plan in your relationship.

If a man decides to build a house, he usually needs to find a builder. He must choose the builder that will be able to meet the wants and needs of his family. As the buyer, he must learn to get to know and trust the builder for the work that he is preparing to do, and the builder will produce different house plans based on what the buyer has expressed he is looking for. When the buyer agrees with the house plan, the builder will get his crew to work on buying materials. He will then start the process of building the house.

Throughout this process, there is one thing that the buyer nor the builder can determine: that is the uncontrollables. Neither the builder nor the buyer can control the weather, material delays, workers being sick, emergencies, etc. It doesn't matter how angry the buyer gets about the uncontrollable things that happen; it still won't change the fact that the deadline may have to change.

In building a relationship, you choose who you want to build your life with. However, you will encounter some uncontrollables, such as misunderstandings and miscommunications. These are things that just happen, especially when other people interfere with your relationship, and unless you are on an island, you will interact with others.

Just because you run into uncontrollable issues or situations along the way doesn't mean that you have chosen the wrong person. This is where communication is key. You have to know your partner well enough not make assumptions about anything. Trust your partner. Instead of a standoff, always give your partner the benefit of the doubt and hear them out for clarity. You may feel how you want to feel about a situation, but don't shut down, close out, ignore, withhold affection, or send your partner to the doghouse. This will only build resentment, bitterness, discontent, and animosity, which will lead to bigger problems. As partners who are striving to build on a solid foundation, eliminate passive-aggressive behaviors that belittle each other. Instead, build each other up with behaviors that encourage.

Another big mistake couples make is playing games with affection. When you have moments of disagreements, never auction, ration, or "play chicken" with your affection. This game of chicken—where whoever is the most offended will withhold affection until their partner relents (cries chicken) or comes up with the highest barter for the affection (auction) by buying gifts or doing something extravagant to get back into the good graces of their partner—is detrimental to a relationship.

Likewise, when a partner uses the rationing method, they are doing something for their partner out of duty and not dedication. There are many aspects of a relationship that could be abused through this kind of behavior, but the main one and the most hurtful one is sex. You should never be satisfied with giving your partner just enough intimacy to get by. By doing this, there is no connection. Intimacy is not just about fulfilling a task or completing a duty. Duty means there's a time limit on my commitment and my obligation to you. Dedication means there are no limits to the lengths I will go to make sure we each have everything we need to be healthy and whole in this relationship. Dedication remembers the vow and honors the commitment that was made at the altar.

When there is a disagreement in a marriage or relationship, both you and your spouse should agree that there will be no mistreatment, neglect, or abuse of the other while trying to come to a resolution. As you work to resolve the issues, this will help you stay out of the doghouse.

The Doghouse Reflections

What type of disagreements or perceived disagreements will cause you to consider the doghouse an option?

How can we disagree in a relationship but not diminish our partner?

THE DOGHOUSE

What resolutions can we come up with to eliminate the option of "the doghouse" in our relationship?

Ask your spouse: What behaviors are non-negotiables in our relationship?

What can each spouse do to recover trust, peace, and unity after a disagreement?

THE HOME OF MARRIAGE

List one thing from this chapter that you can incorporate in your relationship moving forward.

Chapter 14
Date Night

Date night, after many years together, can become a forgotten activity in many marriages and long-term relationships. Yet, date night is essential for the health and wellness of your marriage. It is important to spend time outside of your home. This time away gives you both a chance to disconnect from to-do lists, tasks, chores, and children and focus solely on each other.

Although a candlelight dinner at home is always an option as it is intimate and saves you money, it does not allow the distractions of home life to stay muted. There will always be a phone ringing, a knock at the door, or a child needing attention.

In the beginning of a relationship, it is easy to have date nights and getaways because that is the process by which you are vetting each other. As the years roll along, it's easy for date night to become a distant memory or just another task to add to your to-do list. To prevent this from happening, make time for each other. Even if you have to synchronize your schedules, calendars, and to-do lists, it's important to put time and thought into the activities you decide to do.

Maintaining a consistent date night ensures that you will always make time for your spouse, and it also provides time to check in and stay on the same page as your spouse. Date night helps to cultivate a deeper bond and connection to the one you love and have committed a lifetime to.

As far as frequency, it is up to you and your spouse, but you should base it on the needs of your relationship. Allow for scheduled and spontaneous date nights, especially if you both feel that it's time to bond or reset. Make time anytime your life will allow.

Though date night is not technically a part of The Home of Marriage, it is important to spend time outside the home. Have fun with it. Be creative and customize what you do to your budget. You will find that most things don't require a lot of money, but it requires time equity. The goal is to make sure that whatever you decide to do, give your partner your undivided attention.

Please note: The lack of money should never deter you from connecting with your partner on a close, intimate level. We listed the suggestions in the next section (Date Night Suggestions section) because we had to be creative in making a lot of these ideas work because of where we were financially at certain phases of our lives. We hope that some of these suggestions will help keep the spark in your own marriage.

Date Night Questions

When considering your date night activities, is there something you absolutely are not willing to do?

___

What date night activities or ideas would you like to explore?

DATE NIGHT

Is your idea of date nights more on the stay-cation side or vacation side? Why or why not?

What is on your date night bucket list?

DATE NIGHT

What is your idea of a great date night and a horrible date night?
Note: Karoke may be a terrible idea if your partner is an introvert.

Date Night Suggestions

- Restaurant Crawl: Go to three of your favorite restaurants and order your favorite drinks and appetizers from one, an entrée from another, and dessert and coffee from another.

- Memory Crawl: Revisit the most memorable places from your past together and reminisce or take pictures to make new memories in those spots.

- Go camping or glamping.

- Try an Escape Room (only if you have worked on communication).

- Outdoor Concerts.

- Comedy Shows (it's important to laugh and have light moments often).

- Host a dinner party with friends.

- Couples Spa Day (This can be done at home, too).

- Go to the lake/watch sunset/sunrise.

- Have a picnic.

- Make a couple's bucket list.

List your own suggestions below:

_____
_____
_____
_____
_____

Chapter 15
Parting Advice

It is inevitable that any relationship, whether married, engaged, dating, or just getting to know each other, will face some sort of hardship at one point or another. How you handle the hardship will be the determining factor of whether your relationship survives or not.

We have had the opportunity to witness many successful marriages, but having a successful marriage doesn't relegate or dismiss the reality of hardship. We have been asked, on many occasions, how you all have stayed together all these years successfully. We must admit that it has not been without hardship. We have endured many trials and tribulations, misfortune, distress, and much adversity. It is how we chose to see those situations that made the difference. What you say to each other and what you say about times of affliction can have an impact on the outcome of a hardship.

1 Corinthians 7:13-14a (NKJV) says, "And a woman who has a husband who does not believe, if he is willing to live with her, let her not divorce him. For the unbelieving husband is sanctified by the wife, and the unbelieving wife is sanctified by the husband." In other words, what each of you do in a covenant relationship matters. Many times, we must stay and endure hardships with our spouses because there is always an opportunity for you to win or

lose your spouse with your actions. The Bible is very clear here: a wife sanctifies her unbelieving husband, and a husband sanctifies his unbelieving wife.

In the beginning of our relationship and early marriage years, there was a time when my husband was establishing himself and settling on a career. It was during those times that I was doing well in my career and making a decent amount of money. I never made my husband feel small or unappreciated because of the amount of money that was being brought in. I always tried to assure him that we were in this together and that together, we could get through any hardship.

It was that thinking that allowed us to grow together, stick together, and fight together for what we wanted as a family. When we were able to show this support to each other no matter what situation we faced, we saw ourselves becoming stronger together. Fast forward to today, the same grace that I was willing to give my husband in the earlier years is the same grace he has extended to me throughout the years.

When a couple is having times of adversity, the first response shouldn't be divorce. In many instances, people will try to advise you on what you should and shouldn't deal with, but that is not their decision to make. In these times of challenge, you both should take the time to evaluate your circumstances.

It is not up to anyone outside of your relationship to determine if you stay or go. Staying and supporting your spouse through these times opens up a window to be able to be a good witness to your spouse. It also demonstrates the faith and trust that you have in your spouse and your relationship. These sorts of efforts are what build great relationships and allow you to be able to stand the test of time in a marriage.

One thing that solidified my feelings about my commitment and dedication to my husband was his character of being loyal, dependable, and devoted, even in the earlier years of our marriage.

PARTING ADVICE

In African American communities, we often amplify the myth that our men don't stay, but that's not true. My husband has consistently been a man I can count on, and he stayed and endured through the tough times, and there are many more men out there who will do the same.

It is imperative that you are able to mutually prove that you are supportive of each other and that what you have together is worth the work. I would receive a call every day like clockwork—I could almost set a timer to it—where my husband would call on his lunch break to check in, and I still get those calls to this very day. It's kind of like receiving a subliminal message from your partner, *I'm still here for you and for us.*

If you make goals and promises with your spouse, do everything within your power to meet their expectations. Keep your vows and promises, and when things arise that thwart your plans, make sure you communicate that and move to a different plan.

Our final word of advice that we would like to share with you is, as you make your way through your relationship journey, always be a person that your partner can count on. There are so many things in life that are uncertain, but if your partner has the assurance that no matter what comes or goes, they can count on you, there is nothing in this life that you can't accomplish together.

NOTES

1. The Wizard of Oz, Directed by Victor Fleming, Metro-Goldwyn-Mayer (MGM), 1939.

2. Pendergrass, Teddy. "When Somebody Loves You Back," Life Is a Song Worth Singing, Philadelphia International Records and Sony Music Entertainment, 1978.

3. "What Happens Here, Stays Here." Destination Marketing, Las Vegas Convention and Visitors Authority, https://www.lvcva.com/destination-marketing/advertising-campaigns/what-happens-here-stays-here/. Accessed 24 September 2024.

ABOUT THE AUTHOR

Larry and Leeneen Harris met in the summer of 1982, just before starting high school. They ultimately became high school sweethearts, and their love story continued to blossom, leading to marriage and the joy of welcoming their son. Today, they are proud grandparents to three wonderful grandchildren, Jada, Da'Mauria, and Dy'Jerion, and their commitment to each other has grown through decades of shared life, faith, and family.

For over 30 years, Larry and Leeneen have dedicated their lives to ministry, serving their community with a passion for building strong, faith-filled relationships. Leeneen Harris is an ordained minister, while Larry Harris has faithfully served as an ordained deacon for more than three decades. Together, they are launching a new ministry called Marriage Matters, a platform designed to address the issues of marriage both inside and outside the church.

In addition to his work in ministry, Larry has spent 35 years with Ford Motor Company, where he continues to be employed. His strong work ethic and dedication to both his professional and personal life are a testament to his commitment to family and faith.

Leeneen Harris retired after 25 years as an Operational Manager in Retail Management. Now, she embraces her role as a homemaker and devotes herself fully to ministry, finding joy in serving others and nurturing her family.

Together, Larry and Leeneen hope to inspire couples through their ministry, sharing the lessons they've learned in their own marriage and offering practical wisdom to help others build lasting, fulfilling marriages.

Made in the USA
Middletown, DE
27 October 2024